THE THREE MOST IMPORTANT WORDS IN LIFE ARE

ATTITUDE
ATTITUDE
ATTITUDE

THE THREE MOST IMPORTANT WORDS IN LIFE ARE

ATTITUDE
ATTITUDE
ATTITUDE

EDITED BY MARY G. RODARTE

ARIEL BOOKS

**Andrews McMeel
Publishing**

Kansas City

01 02 03 04 05 WLS 10 9 8 7 6 5 4 3 2 1

The three most important words in life are: attitude, attitude, attitude / edited by Mary G. Rodarte.
    p. cm.
  "Ariel Books."
ISBN 0-7407-1898-3 (pbk.)
  1. Attitude (Psychology)—Quotations, maxims, etc. I. Rodarte, Mary.

BF327 .T48 2001
152.4—dc21

2001033497

Book design and composition by Diane Hobbing

——— ATTENTION: SCHOOLS AND BUSINESS ———

Andrews McMeel books are available at quantity discounts with bulk purchase for educational, business, or sales promotion use. For information, please write to : Special Sales Department, Andrews McMeel Publishing, 4520 Main Street, Kansas City, Missouri 64111.

CONTENTS

THE THREE MOST IMPORTANT WORDS IN LIFE ARE

ATTITUDE
ATTITUDE
ATTITUDE

INTRODUCTION

When a challenge comes your way, how do you respond? Do you see it as a problem or an opportunity? It all depends on your attitude. The importance of your attitude cannot be overstated. Perhaps Charles Swindoll put it best when he wrote:

The longer I live, the more I realize the impact of attitude on life. Attitude, to me, is more important than facts. It is more important than the past, than education, than money, than circumstances, than failure, than successes, than what other people think or say or do. It is more important than appearance, giftedness, or skill. It will make or break a company . . . a church . . . a home. The remarkable thing is we have a choice every day regarding the attitude we will embrace for that day. We cannot change our past . . . we cannot change the inevitable. The only thing we can do is play on the one string we have, and that is our attitude. . . . I am convinced that life is 10% what happens to me and 90% how I react to it. And so it is with you . . . we are in charge of our Attitudes.

To hear from other people with great attitudes, read on . . .

BE
PASSIONATE

Winning isn't everything, but wanting to win is.

—VINCE LOMBARDI, FOOTBALL COACH
(1913-1970)

Look at everything as though you were seeing it either for the first or last time. Then your time on earth will be filled with glory.

—BETTY SMITH, AUTHOR
(1904-1972)

I'll take a smart person with passion over someone with years of experience any day. People with intelligence and passion will get the problem solved, no matter what.

—CAROL BARTZ, PRESIDENT, CHAIRMAN, AND CEO OF
AUTODESK, INC.
(B. 1948)

I'm just going to keep going and going and going until I can't go anymore.

—LARRY BOSSIDY, CHAIRMAN OF ALLIEDSIGNAL, INC.
(B. 1935)

He turns not back who is bound to a star.

—LEONARDO DA VINCI,
ARCHITECT, ENGINEER, PAINTER,
SCULPTOR, AND SCIENTIST
(1452-1519)

The business keeps me fresh because it's something I'm passionate about. It's difficult to stay fresh around something that doesn't inspire you.

—HANS SNOOK, CEO OF ORANGE

There's one surefire way for me to keep moving, stay passionate and avoid going stale. I take it personally—"it" being the imbalances, injustices or irrationalities that I come across every day in my job.

—ANITA RODDICK, FOUNDER AND COCHAIR OF
THE BODY SHOP
(B. 1942)

When what you believe comes from the heart, it gives you the energy and the drive, and generates enthusiasm that's contagious.

—ELIZABETH DOLE, PRESIDENT AND CEO OF
AMERICAN RED CROSS
(B. 1936)

I ask everybody: Didn't you get turned on when you got an A in school? Didn't you get turned on when you were selected for the first team or you got a letter? Didn't you get excited if your marching band won? Okay. It's the same for us. We've got to get to the finals.

—DAVID JOHNSON, CHAIRMAN OF
CAMPBELL SOUP COMPANY
(B. 1932)

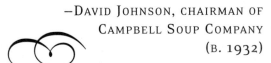

To stay fresh, try to pass on your enjoyment and enthusiasm to everyone else–you get it back.

—MARK STRACHAN, CEO OF GAMEPLAY

I believe a company responds to the passion and enthusiasm of its leaders. It's contagious. If you can't stand there and pour your heart into what you're saying we ought to be doing, then how do you expect others to be passionate?

—HANS BECHERER, CHAIRMAN OF DEERE AND COMPANY
(B. 1935)

I have the most fun job in the world, and love coming to work each day because there are always new challenges, new opportunities, and new things to learn.

—BILL GATES, FOUNDER, CHAIRMAN, AND CEO OF
MICROSOFT CORPORATION
(B. 1955)

Do something you enjoy—music, business, public service, whatever. If [you] don't enjoy going to work, I don't care if [your] IQ is thirty points higher, the guy with the inferior IQ—who loves what he is doing—will beat [you] to death.

—ACE GREENBERG, CHAIRMAN OF THE
EXECUTIVE COMMITTEE AND SENIOR
MANAGING DIRECTOR OF
BEAR STEARNS COMPANIES, INC.
(B. 1927)

I believe you have to make your own opportunity. You really have to get going. Get out! Find 'em! Set 'em up! Do 'em!

—DIANA ROSS, SINGER AND ACTRESS
(B. 1944)

The people—men or women—who are most successful, are people who love what they do and are passionate about it.

—SHELLY LAZARUS, CHAIRMAN AND CEO OF
OGILVY AND MATHER WORLDWIDE
(B. 1947)

If you look at the CEOs who have been successful, they all have incredible passion about their business. If you don't have that, I don't see how you can possibly be a leader.

—CHARLES SCHWAB, FOUNDER, CHAIRMAN, AND CEO OF
THE CHARLES SCHWAB CORPORATION
(B. 1937)

Passion is the engagement of our souls with something beyond us, something that helps us put up with or fight against insurmountable odds, even at high risks, because it is all worth it.

—JANET O. HAGBERG, AUTHOR

If you're interested in something and love what you're doing, it's not stressful.

—SIR MARTIN SORRELL, CEO OF WPP GROUP
(B. 1945)

Don't bunt. Aim out of the ballpark.

—DAVID OGILVY, PRESIDENT OF
OGILVY, BENSON AND MATHER
(1911–1999)

When you put yourself wholeheartedly into something, energy grows. It seems inexhaustible. If, on the other hand, you are divided and conflicted about what you are doing, you create anxiety. And the amount of physical and emotional energy consumed by anxiety is exorbitant.

—HELEN DE ROSIS, AUTHOR

The absolutely fundamental point is that you've got to enjoy what you're doing, and show other people that you're enjoying it. It's important how your work colleagues perceive you. If you are enjoying yourself but not showing it, you won't get the feedback you need.

—MARK STRACHAN, CEO OF GAMEPLAY

There were times when people have looked at the darkness under my eyes—I'm very pale and at the end of days of working on some challenging problem, I will be drained and gray—and they'll say, "You look terrible." And I'll reply, "But I feel terrific." That's the essence of it. I feel terrific. I'm wired, turned on, juices flowing, stretched by the challenge. Excitement surrounds me.

—DAVID JOHNSON, CHAIRMAN OF CAMPBELL SOUP COMPANY
(B. 1932)

Life is a great big canvas, and you should throw all the paint on it you can.

—DANNY KAYE, ACTOR, COMEDIAN, AND SINGER
(1913-1987)

Swing hard, in case they throw the ball where you're swinging.

—DUKE SNIDER, BASEBALL PLAYER

(B. 1926)

WHISTLE
WHILE YOU WORK

A willing heart adds feather to the heel.

—JOANNA BAILLIE, PLAYWRIGHT AND POET
(1762-1851)

Energy is probably the most important thing . . . to have the energy to get up every morning and hit the deck running and run hard all day long.

—BILL MARRIOTT, CHAIRMAN AND PRESIDENT OF
MARRIOTT INTERNATIONAL, INC.
(B. 1932)

Strive for excellence at each place you are in your life at that time.

—MICHAEL EISNER, CHAIRMAN AND CEO OF
THE WALT DISNEY COMPANY
(B. 1942)

I wanted to make a difference. . . . I had this Protestant challenge that says, "To those to whom much is given much is expected." At the end of your days, this world should somehow be better because you passed through it.

—MARTHA INGRAM, CHAIRMAN AND CEO OF
INGRAM INDUSTRIES, INC.
(B. 1935)

The first thing I always say is that within reason, you can accomplish almost anything in life that you want to, as long as you're willing to work hard—and smart—to get it.

—JOHN CHAMBERS, CEO OF CISCO SYSTEMS, INC.
(B. 1949)

My view has always been to try to do the job that I'm in as best I'm able to and do it with an idea of anticipating the job ahead of it. . . . I wanted to make sure I was learning and growing.

—JOHN PEPPER, CHAIRMAN OF
THE PROCTOR AND GAMBLE COMPANY
(B. 1938)

When I got into sales, I said, "How am I ever going to differentiate myself? I'm not as smart as some of these folks, but if they make ten sales calls a day, I'll make twelve. If they work eight hours, I'll work fourteen." Nobody can take away effort, and blood, sweat, tears.

—DANIEL P. TULLY, CHAIRMAN EMERITUS OF
MERRILL LYNCH AND COMPANY
(B. 1932)

The thing that will separate you from everyone else is a combination of innovativeness, creativity, and self-motivation. . . . The people who are going to stand out are those who take the initiative and are self-motivated to anticipate what the next need is, or anticipate how they can be supportive.

—WALTER SHIPLEY, CHAIRMAN OF
CHASE MANHATTAN CORPORATION
(B. 1935)

Nothing is work unless you'd rather be doing something else.

—GEORGE HALAS, FOOTBALL COACH
(1895-1983)

Problems are only opportunities with thorns on them.

—HUGH MILLER, AUTHOR AND GEOLOGIST
(1802-1856)

The best preparation for work is not thinking about work, talking about work, or studying for work: it is work.

—WILLIAM WELD, POLITICIAN
(B. 1945)

You're never as good as everyone tells you when you win, and you're never as bad as they say when you lose.

—LOU HOLTZ, FOOTBALL COACH
(B. 1937)

I'd rather be a failure at something I enjoy than be a success at something I hate.

—GEORGE BURNS, COMEDIAN
(1896-1996)

A problem is a chance for you to do your best.

—DUKE ELLINGTON, JAZZ MUSICIAN
(1899-1974)

If opportunity doesn't knock, build a door.

—MILTON BERLE, ACTOR
(B. 1908)

A man who enjoys responsibility usually gets it. A man who merely likes exercising authority usually loses it.

—MALCOLM S. FORBES, MAGAZINE PUBLISHER
(1919-1990)

It's so much better to greet the world with a smile on your face. You can't show me people with great accomplishments who are negative people. I want to see people who are positive.

—LARRY BOSSIDY, CHAIRMAN OF ALLIEDSIGNAL, INC.
(B. 1935)

The most manifest sign of wisdom is continued cheerfulness.

—MICHEL MONTAIGNE, ESSAYIST AND POLITICIAN
(1533-1592)

TAKE TIME TO SMELL THE FLOWERS

I don't think success is a place or a definition, I think it's a direction. It's very important to look at how you're living your life—and it should be pointed in the right direction.

—CHARLES WANG, FOUNDER, CHAIRMAN, AND CEO OF
COMPUTER ASSOCIATES INTERNATIONAL, INC.
(B. 1944)

Taking joy in living is a woman's best cosmetic.

—ROSALIND RUSSELL, ACTRESS AND PHILANTHROPIST
(1911-1976)

Life is a journey in self-discovery. If we're not growing, we're not living fully.

—SUSAN TAYLOR, JOURNALIST, AUTHOR, AND EDITOR
(B. 1946)

Don't take your holidays for granted. It's a mistake a lot of people make, but you need them. And don't take the mobile phone with you.

—Sir George Russell, chairman of 3i and Camelot

The important thing is not to stop questioning. Curiosity has its own reason for existing. One cannot help but be in awe when he contemplates the mysteries of eternity, of life, of the marvelous structure of reality. It is enough if one tries merely to comprehend a little of this mystery every day. Never lose a holy curiosity.

—ALBERT EINSTEIN, PHYSICIST
(1879-1955)

Butterflies count not months but moments, and yet have time enough.

—RABINDRANATH TAGORE, AUTHOR AND PHILOSOPHER
(1861-1941)

You must take your holiday—we kick people out of the door here if they don't take it.

—MARK STRACHAN, CEO OF GAMEPLAY

The time to relax is when you don't have time for it.

—SYDNEY J. HARRIS, JOURNALIST AND AUTHOR
(1917-1986)

All the art of living lies in a fine mingling of letting go and holding on.

—HAVELOCK ELLIS, PSYCHOLOGIST
(1859-1939)

Do not take life too seriously. You will never get out of it alive.

—ELBERT HUBBARD, AUTHOR
(1856-1915)

A list is my bible for the day—it tells me what I haven't done and what there still is for me to do. I always have a breakfast meeting at eight—a very good way of starting the day. I work through my list religiously, and I don't work late at night.

—BARBARA THOMAS, CHAIRMAN OF WHITWORTHS
AND COFOUNDER OF NET INVESTOR

There is more to life than increasing its speed.

—MOHANDAS K. GANDHI, NATIONALIST AND SPIRITUAL LEADER
(1869-1948)

If you had to choose only two qualities to get you through times of change, the first should be a sense of self-worth and the second a sense of humor.

—JENNIFER JAMES, AUTHOR AND MOTIVATIONAL SPEAKER

If you treat every situation as a life-and-death matter, you'll die a lot of times.

—DEAN SMITH, COLLEGE BASKETBALL COACH
(B. 1931)

To live only for some future goal is shallow. It's the sides of the mountain that sustain life, not the top.

—ROBERT M. PIRSIG, AUTHOR
(B. 1928)

In the era of the internet and e-mail everything's running at a far greater speed. That's a danger. Letters take a day or two to arrive, allowing things to calm down a bit.

—Sir George Russell, chairman of 3i and Camelot

We have as much time as we need.

—MELODY BEATTIE, AUTHOR AND COUNSELOR
(B. 1948)

He who can no longer pause to wonder and stand rapt in awe is as good as dead; his eyes are closed.

—ALBERT EINSTEIN, PHYSICIST
(1879-1955)

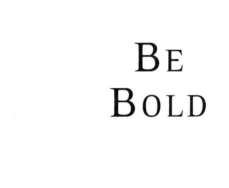

BE
BOLD

It's better to be a lion for a day than a sheep all your life.

—SISTER KENNY, NUN AND NURSE
(1880-1952)

When you cannot make up your mind which of two evenly balanced courses of action you should take—choose the bolder.

—W. J. SLIM, GOVERNOR-GENERAL OF AUSTRALIA
(1891-1970)

It has been my philosophy of life that difficulties vanish when faced boldly.

—ISAAC ASIMOV, AUTHOR AND SCIENTIST
(1920-1992)

Invariably, the mistakes you look back on with regret involve situations where you played it too safe.

—MIKE VOLKEMA, PRESIDENT AND CEO OF
HERMAN MILLER, INC.
(B. 1955)

We're face-to-face with our destiny. And we must meet it with a high and resolute courage, for ours is the life of action, of strenuous performance, of duty. Let us live in the harness of striving mightily. Let us run the risk of wearing out rather than rusting out.

—THEODORE ROOSEVELT, U.S. PRESIDENT
(1858-1919)

If you're never scared or embarrassed or hurt, it means you never take any chances.

—JULIA SOREL, AUTHOR
(B. 1926)

Fear goes out and energy rises, and things get done.

—ALEX TROTMAN, CHAIRMAN AND CEO OF
FORD MOTOR COMPANY
(B. 1933)

Take a chance! All life is a chance. The man who goes furthest is generally the one who is willing to do and dare.

—DALE CARNEGIE, LECTURER AND AUTHOR
(1888-1955)

The greatest mistake you can make in life is continually to be fearing you will make one.

—ELBERT HUBBARD, AUTHOR
(1856-1915)

All serious daring starts from within.

—EUDORA WELTY, NOVELIST
(B. 1909)

What would life be if we had no courage to attempt anything?

—Vincent van Gogh, painter
(1853-1890)

Not everything that is faced can be changed. But nothing can be changed until it is faced.

—JAMES BALDWIN, NOVELIST AND CIVIL RIGHTS ACTIVIST
(1924-1987)

The spirit, the will to win, and the will to excel are the things that endure. These qualities are so much more important than the events that occur.

—VINCE LOMBARDI, FOOTBALL COACH
(1913–1970)

The difference between those who make it and those who don't rests in the ability to make difficult choices.

—LAUREN GREGG, ASSISTANT COACH OF
THE U.S. WOMEN'S NATIONAL SOCCER TEAM

What are the motivating factors for me? It's the commitment to the vision, being open to new ideas, not being afraid to experiment.

—HANS SNOOK, CEO OF ORANGE

All my life I have gone out on a limb, but I have turned the limb into a bridge, and there is cool, clear water flowing under.

—HOLLY NEAR, SINGER AND SONGWRITER
(B. 1949)

The most vital quality a soldier can possess is self-confidence.

—GEORGE S. PATTON, U.S. ARMY GENERAL
(1885-1945)

Whatis more mortifying than to feel that you have missed the plum for want of courage to shake the tree?

—LOGAN PEARSALL SMITH, AUTHOR AND ESSAYIST
(1865-1946)

We're all capable of climbing so much higher than we usually permit ourselves to suppose.

—OCTAVIA BUTLER, SCIENCE-FICTION AUTHOR
(B. 1947)

Never let the fear of striking out get in your way.

–BABE RUTH, BASEBALL PLAYER
(1895-1948)

Use what talents you possess: the woods would be very silent if no birds sang there except those that sang best.

—HENRY VAN DYKE, AUTHOR AND CLERGYMAN
(1852–1933)

Determine that the thing can and shall be done, and then we shall find the way.

—ABRAHAM LINCOLN, U.S. PRESIDENT
(1809-1865)

If you're not failing now and again, it's a sign you're playing it safe.

—WOODY ALLEN, FILMMAKER
(B. 1935)

It takes as much courage to have tried and failed as it does to have tried and succeeded.

—ANNE MORROW LINDBERGH, AUTHOR AND AVIATOR
(1906-2001)

The opportunities of man are limited only by his imagination. But so few have imagination that there are ten thousand fiddlers to one composer.

—CHARLES F. KETTERING, AUTOMOBILE ENGINEER
(1876-1958)

What great thing would you attempt if you knew you could not fail?

—Robert H. Schuller, author and clergyman
(b. 1926)

TAKE
CONTROL

I couldn't wait for success ... so I went ahead without it.

—JONATHAN WINTERS, COMEDIAN
(B. 1925)

How a person masters his fate is more important than what his fate is.

—WILHELM VON HUMBOLDT, DIPLOMAT AND PHILOLOGIST
(1767-1835)

The difference between a successful person and others is not a lack of strength, not a lack of knowledge, but rather in a lack of will.

—Vince Lombardi, football coach
(1913-1970)

You don't get to choose how you're going to die. Or when. You can only decide how you're going to live. Now.

—JOAN BAEZ, FOLKSINGER AND PACIFIST
(B. 1941)

Nothing great will ever be achieved without great men, and men are great only if they are determined to be so.

—CHARLES DE GAULLE, FRENCH PRESIDENT
(1890-1970)

K nowing who you are begins in the mind.

—BEBE MOORE CAMPBELL, AUTHOR

Everything comes to he who hustles while he waits.

—THOMAS A. EDISON, INVENTOR
(1847-1931)

Don't wait around for other people to be happy for you. Any happiness you get you've got to make yourself.

—ALICE WALKER, AUTHOR
(B. 1944)

The summit of happiness is reached when a person is ready to be what he is.

—ERASMUS, HUMANIST AND SCHOLAR
(c. 1466-1536)

God asks no man whether he will accept life. That is not the choice. One must take it. The only choice is how.

—HENRY WARD BEECHER, CLERGYMAN AND ORATOR
(1813-1887)

Don't put off for tomorrow what you can do today, because if you enjoy it today you can do it again tomorrow.

—JAMES A. MICHENER, AUTHOR
(1907-1997)

Success is getting what you want. Happiness is liking what you get.

—H. JACKSON BROWN JR., AUTHOR
(B. 1940)

Don't be afraid of failing. It doesn't matter how many times you fall down. All that matters is how many times you keep getting up.

—MARIAN WRIGHT EDELMAN, LAWYER AND FOUNDER OF
CHILDREN'S DEFENSE FUND
(B. 1939)

Success is not forever, and failure's not fatal.

—DON SHULA, FOOTBALL PLAYER AND COACH
(B. 1930)

There is no comparison between that which is lost by not succeeding and that which is lost by not trying.

—FRANCIS BACON, STATESMAN AND PHILOSOPHER
(1561-1626)

Ability is what you're capable of doing. Motivation determines what you do. Attitude determines how well you do it.

—LOU HOLTZ, FOOTBALL COACH
(B. 1937)

Everybody thinks of changing humanity and nobody thinks of changing himself.

—LEO TOLSTOY, NOVELIST
(1823-1910)

People often say that this or that person has not yet found himself. But the self is not something that one finds. It is something one creates.

—THOMAS SZASZ, AUTHOR AND PSYCHIATRIST
(B. 1920)

Self-pity in its early stages is as snug as a feather mattress.
Only when it hardens does it become uncomfortable.

—MAYA ANGELOU, AUTHOR AND POET
(B. 1928)

In the depth of winter I finally learned that there was in me an invincible summer.

—ALBERT CAMUS, AUTHOR AND PHILOSOPHER
(1913-1960)

Never feel self-pity, the most destructive emotion there is. How awful to be caught up in the terrible squirrel cage of self.

—MILLICENT FENWICK, POLITICIAN
(1910-1992)

Wherever we look upon this earth, the opportunities take shape within the problems.

—NELSON A. ROCKEFELLER, U.S. VICE PRESIDENT
(1908-1979)

You are in charge of your own attitude.

—MARIAN WRIGHT EDELMAN, LAWYER AND FOUNDER OF
CHILDREN'S DEFENSE FUND
(B. 1939)

Most human beings have an almost infinite capacity for taking things for granted.

—ALDOUS HUXLEY, NOVELIST, CRITIC, AND ESSAYIST
(1894-1963)

Don't find fault. Find a remedy.

—HENRY FORD, AUTOMOBILE MANUFACTURER
(1863-1947)

It's a funny thing about life; if you refuse to accept anything but the best, you very often get it.

—W. SOMERSET MAUGHAM, NOVELIST AND DRAMATIST
(1874-1965)

The more mistakes I made, the faster I learned.

—MICHAEL DELL, FOUNDER, CHAIRMAN, AND CEO OF
DELL COMPUTER CORPORATION

Happiness is mostly a by-product of doing what makes us feel fulfilled.

—BENJAMIN SPOCK, PHYSICIAN AND AUTHOR
(B. 1903)

Mistakes are the usual bridge between inexperience and wisdom.

—PHYLLIS THEROUX, AUTHOR
(B. 1939)

Lord, where we are wrong, make us willing to change; where we are right, make us easy to live with.

—PETER MARSHALL, CLERGYMAN
(1902-1949)

NEVER
GIVE
UP

You're never a loser until you quit trying.

—MIKE DITKA, FOOTBALL PLAYER AND COACH
(B. 1939)

A certain amount of opposition is a great help to a man. Kites rise against, not with the wind.

—JOHN NEAL, AUTHOR
(1793-1876)

Never give in—in nothing, great or small, large or petty—except to convictions of honor and good sense.

—WINSTON CHURCHILL, STATESMAN
(1874-1965)

Ｗe may encounter many defeats but we must not be defeated.

—MAYA ANGELOU, AUTHOR AND POET
(B. 1928)

When things are bad, we take comfort in the thought that they could always be worse. And when they are, we find hope in the thought that things are so bad they have to get better.

—MALCOLM S. FORBES, MAGAZINE PUBLISHER
(1919-1990)

Although the world is full of suffering, it is also full of the overcoming of it.

—HELEN KELLER, AUTHOR
(1880-1968)

Defeat may serve as well as victory to shake the soul and let the glory out.

—EDWIN MARKHAM, POET
(1852-1940)

We must accept finite disappointment, but we must never lose infinite hope.

—MARTIN LUTHER KING JR., CIVIL RIGHTS LEADER
(1929-1968)

Your life is filled with possibility. Reach high, look forward, and never give up. The world is waiting for you.

—MARIAN WRIGHT EDELMAN, LAWYER AND FOUNDER OF
CHILDREN'S DEFENSE FUND
(B. 1939)

Wisely, and slow. They stumble that run fast.

—WILLIAM SHAKESPEARE, PLAYWRIGHT AND POET
(1564-1616)

There are no secrets to success. It is the result of preparation, hard work, learning from failure.

—COLIN L. POWELL, U.S. ARMY OFFICER AND STATESMAN
(B. 1937)

The difference between the impossible and the possible lies in a person's determination.

–TOMMY LASORDA, BASEBALL PLAYER AND MANAGER
(B. 1927)

What we need are more people who specialize in the impossible.

—THEODORE ROETHKE, POET
(1908-1963)

The way I see it, if you want the rainbow, you gotta put up with the rain.

—DOLLY PARTON, SINGER AND SONGWRITER
(B. 1946)

Perseverance is important.... You have to think "Well, we're just going to keep at it. That is critical."

—STEVE CASE, COFOUNDER, CHAIRMAN, AND CEO OF
AMERICA ONLINE, INC.
(B. 1958)

I think we need to be careful that we don't become self-satisfied. We can't become complacent. We need to keep pressing ourselves to improve to reach levels that other people can't imagine.

—PAUL O'NEILL, TREASURY SECRETARY TO GEORGE W. BUSH
(B. 1935)

A mistake is simply another way of doing things.

—KATHARINE GRAHAM, NEWSPAPER PUBLISHER
(B. 1917)

The easy part is when you have ninety thousand people cheering you on in a soccer stadium. What matters is who you are in those moments when no one is watching.

—LAUREN GREGG, ASSISTANT COACH OF
THE U.S. WOMEN'S NATIONAL SOCCER TEAM

I'm not a good down-time person.

—JILL BARAD, PRESIDENT OF MATTEL, INC.
(B. 1951)

There's nothing final about a mistake, except its being taken as final.

—PHYLLIS BOTTOME, AUTHOR
(1884-1963)

Failure is only the opportunity to begin again more intelligently.

—HENRY FORD, AUTOMOBILE MANUFACTURER
(1863-1947)

It's not whether you get knocked down, it's whether you get up.

—Vince Lombardi, football coach
(1913-1970)

BE
A
LEADER

A leader is someone who can take a group of people to a place they don't think they can go.

—BOB EATON, CHAIRMAN AND CO-CEO OF
DAIMLERCHRYSLER CORPORATION
(B. 1940)

The great thing in this world is not so much where we stand as in what direction we are moving.

—OLIVER WENDELL HOLMES SR., PHYSICIAN, POET, AND ESSAYIST
(1809-1894)

High expectations are the key to everything.

—SAM WALTON, FOUNDER OF WAL-MART STORES
(1918-1992)

It's easy to make a buck. It's a lot tougher to make a difference.

—TOM BROKAW, BROADCAST JOURNALIST
(B. 1940)

The better we feel about ourselves, the fewer times we have to knock somebody else down to feel tall.

—ODETTA, SINGER AND MUSICIAN
(B. 1930)

Whenever I meet someone, I try to imagine him wearing an invisible sign that says: MAKE ME FEEL IMPORTANT! I respond to this sign immediately, and it works wonders.

—MARY KAY ASH, FOUNDER OF MARY KAY COSMETICS
(B. 1918)

People who succeed speak well of themselves to themselves.

—LAURIE BETH JONES, AUTHOR

The key to the whole thing? We do things right. We treat our clients right and we treat each other with dignity and respect.... Do what's right for people, and all of a sudden you will develop a lot of clients and you will be awash in profits. It never works the other way around.

—DANIEL P. TULLY, CHAIRMAN AND CEO OF
MERRILL LYNCH AND COMPANY
(B. 1939)

Leadership: the art of getting someone else to do something you want done because he wants to do it.

—DWIGHT D. EISENHOWER, U.S. PRESIDENT
(1890-1969)

I didn't always listen to others. I thought I was invincible. My ego got a little too big for me.

—WALLY AMOS, FOUNDER OF
FAMOUS AMOS CHOCOLATE COOKIE CO.
(B. 1936)

The best leaders have to be good followers as well. You have to be willing to accept other people's ideas, even when they are in conflict with your own. You have to be willing to subjugate your ego to the needs of your business. You have to be selfless and take risks for your people . . .

—HERB KELLEHER, FOUNDER, CHAIRMAN, AND CEO OF
SOUTHWEST AIRLINES COMPANY
(B. 1931)

Millions of micromoments can add up to victory, and the ability to make small decisions helps you when you need to make the big ones.

—LAUREN GREGG, ASSISTANT COACH OF
THE U.S. WOMEN'S NATIONAL SOCCER TEAM

The successful leaders are people who feel enormous ownership of what they're doing.

—JOHN PEPPER, CHAIRMAN OF
THE PROCTOR AND GAMBLE COMPANY
(B. 1938)

Management is what used to be required to run a company. Today it's leadership. A manager basically controls, establishes plans, makes a budget, allocates work, and tracks results. A leader is much more focused on vision and beliefs. He or she inspires people and breaks roadblocks so that people can accomplish more.

—BOB EATON, CHAIRMAN AND CO-CEO OF
DAIMLERCHRYSLER CORPORATION
(B. 1940)

My mother is 97 and when I get to be her age, the question is going to be, "What did I stand for? Did I make a positive difference for others?" That is what is going to matter, not all of the other more shallow things.

—ELIZABETH DOLE, PRESIDENT AND CEO OF
AMERICAN RED CROSS
(B. 1936)

Everybody's got weaknesses. And if you focus on his or her weaknesses, you're just going to make everybody unhappy. Focus on their strengths.

—BILL STEERE, CHAIRMAN AND CEO OF PFIZER INC.
(B. 1936)

Sandwich every bit of criticism between two heavy layers of praise.

—MARY KAY ASH, FOUNDER OF MARY KAY COSMETICS
(B. 1918)

I think it's . . . important to recognize that success itself motivates. It's very critical that the CEO crafts plans that lead to successful performance for the corporation. You've got to be so careful about that because you can destroy the attitude of everybody in the company. Nobody wants to be part of a loser.

—BOB TILLMAN, CHAIRMAN, PRESIDENT, AND CEO OF
LOWE'S COMPANIES, INC.
(B. 1943)

A rock pile ceases to be a rock pile the moment a single man contemplates it, bearing within him the image of a cathedral.

—ANTOINE DE SAINT-EXUPÉRY, AUTHOR AND AVIATOR
(1900-1944)

It is important as a leader to play to your strengths and not try to be somebody that you're not.

—Sandy Weill, chairman and co-CEO of
Citigroup, Inc.
(b. 1933)

I've learned it's all about teamwork. It's not about what I can do, but what we can do together.

—WALLY AMOS, FOUNDER OF
FAMOUS AMOS CHOCOLATE COOKIE CO.
(B. 1936)

To be a successful person . . . you have to have integrity. Your word has to be worth everything you've got. You must have a moral compass. . . . People will get a sense of you, and if you are not true, you may not feel the effect today, this week, this month, this year, but it will get out.

—CHARLES WANG, FOUNDER, CHAIRMAN, AND CEO OF
COMPUTER ASSOCIATES INTERNATIONAL, INC.
(B. 1944)

THE THREE MOST
IMPORTANT WORDS
IN LIFE ARE
ATTITUDE, ATTITUDE,
ATTITUDE

The greatest discovery of my generation is that a human being can alter his life by altering his attitude.

—WILLIAM JAMES, PHILOSOPHER AND PSYCHOLOGIST
(1842-1910)

A cup is useful only when it is empty; and a mind that is filled with beliefs, with dogmas, with assertions, with quotations is really an uncreative mind.

—J. KRISHNAMURTI, MYSTIC AND SPIRITUALIST
(1895-1986)

He who cannot change the very fabric of his thought will never be able to change reality.

—ANWAR EL-SADAT, PRESIDENT OF EGYPT
(1918–1981)

We look for attitude. . . . It's wonderful to have somebody with a good education, don't misunderstand me. And it's wonderful to have someone who has experience, and maybe even some expertise, but if they have a lousy attitude, we don't want them. . . . [T]he one thing that you cannot change is attitude. We hire for attitude and teach skills if we have to.

—HERB KELLEHER, FOUNDER, CHAIRMAN, AND CEO OF
SOUTHWEST AIRLINES COMPANY
(B. 1931)

All you can do is the best you can. Stay on the balls of your feet as you might in a tennis game. Be ready to change directions if you need to . . .

—MARTHA INGRAM, CHAIRMAN AND CEO OF
INGRAM INDUSTRIES, INC.
(B. 1935)

The mind is its own place, and in itself can make a heaven of hell, a hell of heaven.

—JOHN MILTON, POET AND AUTHOR
(1608-1674)

There are no menial jobs, only menial attitudes.

—WILLIAM J. BENNETT, AUTHOR AND STATESMAN
(B. 1943)

Always laugh at yourself first—before others do.

—ELSA MAXWELL, COLUMNIST AND SOCIALITE
(1883-1963)

The guy with the most resources doesn't win. The guy who utilizes his resources best wins.

−CHUCK KNIGHT, CHAIRMAN OF
EMERSON ELECTRIC COMPANY
(B. 1936)

The kind of beauty I want most is the hard-to-get kind that comes from within—strength, courage, dignity.

—RUBY DEE, ACTRESS AND POET
(B. 1923)

Happy is the person who can laugh at himself. He will never cease to be amused.

—HABIB BOURGUIBA, TUNISIAN PRESIDENT
(B. 1903)

I don't think of all the misery but of the beauty that still remains.

—ANNE FRANK, DIARIST
(1929-1945)

Some people are always grumbling that roses have thorns; I am thankful that thorns have roses.

—ALPHONSE KARR, JOURNALIST AND NOVELIST
(1808-1890)

I f you're going to be able to look back on something and laugh about it, you might as well laugh about it now.

—MARIE OSMOND, SINGER AND COHOST OF TELEVISION SHOW
(B. 1959)

Most of the shadows of this life are caused by our standing in our own sunshine.

—RALPH WALDO EMERSON, POET
(1803-1882)

One of the advantages of being disorderly is that one is constantly making exciting discoveries.

—A. A. MILNE, AUTHOR
(1882-1956)

Failure is the condiment that gives success its flavor.

–TRUMAN CAPOTE, WRITER
(1924-1984)

A man is but a product of his thoughts; what he thinks, that he becomes.

—MOHANDAS K. GANDHI, NATIONALIST AND SPIRITUAL LEADER
(1869-1948)

He that is of a merry heart hath a continual feast.

−Proverbs 15:15

Thoughts are energy. And you can make your world or break your world by your thinking.

—SUSAN TAYLOR, JOURNALIST, AUTHOR, AND EDITOR
(B. 1946)

Change your thoughts and you change your world.

—NORMAN VINCENT PEALE, AUTHOR AND CLERGYMAN
(1898-1993)